MW01233015

Don Jackson's
Prodigal

PRODIGAL

LEAVING CHURCH AND FINDING GOD

DON JACKSON

Prodigal

Leaving Church and Finding God

Don Jackson

ISBN (Print Edition): 979-8-35092-716-0
ISBN (eBook Edition): 979-8-35090-109-2

TABLE OF CONTENTS

INTRODUCTION

IN THE BEGINNING...

There are a hundred ways to finish that sentence, and if I had to put money on it, I'd give myself pretty good odds on guessing how you'd choose to. If you grew up in the same world I did, I bet I'd get my money back.

Maybe the word that ought to come after those first powerful three *is* God. Maybe that's what we want to call it. God. A Higher Power. Consciousness. Thought. Existence. *Life*. But that's the big thing, my friends. In the beginning, there were no limits.

There was nothing but possibility.

Then, life began and humans flooded into the world with a little thing called anxiety. And because we have a need for order, for borders and rules, we decided right away that we ought to put it all into a box, and we named it "Adam and Eve."

How does the old story go? I say that as though I don't know the answer, like I can't recite it verse by verse. I cut my teeth on the story of two folks naked in a garden, eating the forbidden fruit and dooming all of mankind. I lived my life for years as though all of that was real. As though it *mattered*. A world created in 144 hours. A man, and the woman built from his rib. A love story built on scarcity. Eve gets tempted by the serpent and eats from the tree she was barred from, and she gives it to Adam, and bang. That's it for eternal life. We are doomed to death. And from then on, every word in black and white—red and white once you hit the New Testament and Jesus starts talking—is easy to accept as literal. Accepting the truly bizarre becomes the most natural thing in the world.

Once I accepted that all of evolution happened in six days and that the entire human population was born of two humans—just two—, once I accepted the impossible things embedded in the story of creation taken literally, it was easy to accept everything else, and to take it at face value.

It was easy to accept that if my pastor said good kids went to Heaven and bad ones burned in a fiery pit, well that must be true. It was easy to believe that God, the big bearded man in the sky—had created billions and billions of humans, the intricacy of earth, the whole of its history, and determined a single path by which they wouldn't be consumed in the end. That the slightest misstep ripped them off the path of righteousness and sent them hurtling toward damnation. More than that, I guess at the root of it? It was easy to accept that we, as people, are divided.

That we are not one. We are in it for ourselves. There is me and you. There is us and there is them.

All of that fell apart like sand in my hands when I realized that *in the beginning*, I was wrong.

It was never supposed to be taken literally, and of course it wasn't. Adam and Eve aren't players in a story about two humans who ruined it for the rest of us! Adam isn't even there to represent man and Eve woman. That's still division. Divide based on gender or race or status, whatever you will, and it's *still* division.

Adam and Eve, together, represent humanity.

There's not value in reading a story from thousands of years ago about a couple folks who decided to eat some fruit from a magic tree.

There *is* value in reading a story about humanity and letting it seep into your spirit.

Back in the day, people talked in stories. We still do it, and I'm going to do it here. That's what every religion with a creation story has done, and it's exactly what the writers of the Bible did.

It was never supposed to be literal.

Adam and Eve are meant to tell us about the rise of life, about what it means to be human. About what happened when people split off from the life we all shared together at the beginning of all things, and what happened when we grew up. When we chose knowledge, chose to grow, and fell into adulthood, into existence.

Existence is vibrant and beautiful and painful. It's communal and it's lonely. It's everything you read in those first few chapters of Genesis. But if you read it word-for-word, take everything literally, you miss it.

You miss *everything* that matters.

And like I did, you take those absurdities for truth, and everything else is easy to accept.

Let's not do ourselves a disservice and accept that anymore.

I don't want a storybook; I want *truth*.

I don't want division; I want unity.

I don't want a world like the one Adam and Eve fell into—the divided, rocky one we live in now. I want one that looks like possibility again. And if we accept, first, that these spiritual play-by-plays, the books that nations have fought wars over and spilled blood over, are not meant to be dissected, but meant to be absorbed for their universal truths about humanity, then… then that becomes a world that maybe one day we can live in.

Because the truth—the *real* truth of the matter—is that I am not my own. I am not alone, and neither are you. Our natural state is not separation from one another. It is not fighting, not walking alone like we do divided out into billions of people who hate each other.

In the beginning was not you.

It was not me.

In the beginning was we.

PART ONE:

THEN

CHAPTER ONE

MY FATHER MADE HIS LIVING IN REFINEMENT BY FIRE.

He was a welder by trade, and a young minister of the gospel when he went looking for a different way to shape the world. We lived in New Orleans for most of my young childhood, me and my parents and my five siblings. You're thinking, *Big family*. You're right.

I liked New Orleans; we all did. I guess I didn't know how *not* to like it, it was all I knew. If you were a Black family at that time, you went to church, so we did, too. We went to church every Sunday and lived our lives by the breath of God, and my parents were a little tired by me, I think, for always asking questions no one had the answers to—even as a little kid. But for the most part, everything was smooth.

Then things started to go south. It seemed like everyone in the neighborhood was getting pregnant or walking away from someone who was or trying to figure out how to bring up a new life when they were still being brought up themselves. And if there's one thing that terrifies parents, it's the idea of their kids having sex. So we moved.

And I don't mean to a new neighborhood, I mean across the country. When I was seven years old, we picked up our lives and moved from New Orleans, Louisiana to Tulsa, Oklahoma to escape. We didn't know anyone in the state but my uncle and aunt, and that didn't matter. We were starting over.

Business went as usual in Tulsa—as usual as a cross-country move makes things. Church was a million times a week, and we were broke, but we were living. Then, when I was fifteen, my dad announced that he was going to be a preacher. It didn't matter that he didn't have a Bible degree, didn't have credentials. He had heart, and he knew the Bible cover to cover. More than that, when my dad said he was going to do something, he did it. And we were going to build a church.

It was a good time to be a preacher. In that era of the world, especially in the Bible belt, preachers were respected in the community. If you were a teacher or a councilman or trading in the Word of God, folks tipped their hat to you when you walked by. That worked for my dad, and it worked pretty well for us, too.

Well, it worked for *most* of us.

I couldn't seem to get it together.

Couldn't seem to untangle all the questions in my head that had woven themselves into a ball of barbed wire. They made it impossible to go to church on Sunday and every day again after school and soak in it, like all my siblings did.

I think my family looked at the old building my dad preached out of and saw possibility. They saw hope. They saw what our lives, what the community, what the *world* could become if they just put in a little elbow grease and kept the faith.

I'd shut my eyes tight and hope that when I opened them, that mirage would show up for me too. But it never did. What I saw was right in front of me.

I saw a building made of bricks. I saw the time I had to hang out with my friends, to play ball, to do *anything* outside those chapel doors, slipping away second by second and no route by which to get it back and stop it flowing.

More than anything, I saw my family working. I saw my father uproot our whole lives and preach and teach and do everything—*everything*—he was supposed to do. And we were still struggling to get by.

I remember asking my parents about it, because try as I might, I was never the kind of kid who could let things go. I'd say, "Look at that family going to church. Doing right. Coming home to that big brick house. I bet their kids can play sports. I bet they can afford real music lessons. I bet they don't mess with hand-me-downs or stuff from the Goodwill. They're the ones *stocking* the Goodwill."

My parents didn't like that line of thinking. They told me I wasn't supposed to think about that kind of stuff. That didn't matter. What those families were building was temporary; what we were building was eternal. God cared about each of the little birds in the air and clothed the flowers of the grass in splendor. We were worth more than many sparrows![1]

I shouldn't worry.

I'd ask why we were doing all we could, and the white folks down the road had it *all*, and we still had to leave the last bit of milk in the carton for our baby brother every week. If all of this was real, why couldn't we just buy another gallon of milk?

My mom would say, "Don," and Jesus would come out of her mouth.

> *Why do you worry about clothes? See how the flowers of the field grow. They do not labor or spin. Yet I tell you that not even Solomon in all his splendor was dressed like one of these. If that is how God clothes the grass of the field, which is here today and tomorrow is thrown into the fire, will he not much more clothe you—you of little faith? So do not worry, saying, 'What shall we eat?' or 'What shall we drink?' or 'What shall we wear?' For the pagans run after all these things, and your heavenly Father knows*

---

1   Matthew 10:31—NIV

that you need them. But seek first his kingdom and his
righteousness, and all these things will be given to you as
well. Therefore do not worry about tomorrow, for tomor-
row will worry about itself. Each day has enough trouble
of its own. [2]

Oh me of little faith. But I didn't see how I was supposed to have faith when I could look right in my closet and see how low we were running. When the common refrain, even with my dad working himself to the bone outside the house and my mom running herself ragged in it, was, "No, we can't afford that."

We weren't starving, the electric was always on and we always had hot water. We were surviving. But we weren't *thriving*. And here they were, asking me to look past what I could touch, what was real, what was right in front of my face, and see possibility. But possibility didn't buy me new shoes.

As far as I could tell, seeking first his kingdom and his righteousness hadn't gotten us shit. And those questions just kept coming. Our church kept growing, and that just meant more people for me to ask my questions in front of in Sunday school, more opportunities to get kicked out.

Where are all the Black people in prosperity around here, huh?

Who around me is thriving?

If God is so big, why can't he fix all of this mess around me?

You're telling me he can? But he DOESN'T? Why? He's supposed to be the benevolent Big Man in the sky! He doesn't care? Is that it?

I made a teenage career out of getting kicked out of Sunday school.

My parents weren't happy.

I went with them faithfully, showed up to church every day of my life and did what I had to do. I even played in the band—I was a drummer and

---

2   Matthew 6:28-34—NIV.

I loved it. But every one of them knew that under my skin, I was *itching* to get away.

I guess preacher's kids go one of two ways: they grow up perfect or they grow up wild. All five of my siblings went with the former. The Prodigal was me.

They approached things with a Heavenly mindset. I approached my life as a calculus. I was in the seventh grade when my dad took up preaching, and by the time high school came around, I'd refined my way of thinking.

Should I break this rule? wasn't a question of ethics. It was a question of practicality and worth. I wasn't getting out of the house to go drink with my friends or cruise around town or get into *worldly shenanigans.* Absolutely not! And if you thought a single one of us was getting into a school dance? *That* den of sex and iniquity and shoulder pads and puff sleeves? Think again.

It was enough to stop the rest of them.

It wasn't enough to stop me.

I'd think on every little choice in my life, and this was the formula I'd run: 1) How bad did I want it? 2) How likely was I to get caught? 3) If I did, would it be worth it?

Sometimes, it was.

Night of the homecoming dance, I had a suit and a boutonniere and a girl, and by God, it was worth it. So I slipped out of the house and I danced my heart out and I kissed the girl and I spent a few hours acting like I was a regular kid.

My dad was waiting for me when I got home; he always would. It was like the man had a Don alarm. He'd wait in the living room with a Bible and a belt in his hands and lock the doors so I couldn't slip inside, and I knew an ass-whooping was coming.

But I had a tree outside my window. I learned I could climb it and clamber inside my window and be snug under my covers before he knew it.

Hours would pass until he'd crack and be dumbfounded once again.

He'd burst into my room, shouting, "How on *earth* did you get in here? This is impossible."

I'd shrug. "Dad, I don't know what you're talking about. I've been here."

And boy, did *that* set him off.

Again and again. Leaving and coming back around. That was me. One foot out the door, two if I could get by with it, leaving both my faithful parents and my faithful siblings floundering.

They even set up my little brother to keep an eye on me. He didn't have much of a choice; you're a little kid and your parents tell you it's your job to watch after your big brother, make sure to keep him out of trouble and inside the fold, well—you're the big man on campus now. You're gonna do it.

And he did.

My baby brother was a narc.

That was it; that was childhood. Young adulthood, whatever you want to call it.

The point is, I spent a kid's lifetime in a pen, finding a hundred ways to break out.

If I was destined to live life as a sheep, then I was going to be the one that wandered.

And I didn't need a shepherd, Good or otherwise, to come looking for me.

CHAPTER TWO

IT'S FUNNY, LOOKING BACK, TO PICK OUT THE THINGS THAT *REALLY* hurt. Maybe "funny" isn't the right word. Strange? Painful? Not like a sledgehammer, like sandpaper, the way coarse grit could take off your skin—slow and steady, and before you realize it, you're bleeding. Striations in the muscle showing through.

For me, you'd think that would be the ass whoopings, right? I'm not talking abuse, not really. But they happened, and that stuff gets to a person. That's what the psychologists say. Maybe it would be the knowledge that out of all of them, *I* was the only one who needed an eye kept on him. The only one destined for an eternity filled with sulfur. But that's not it. That's not the Big One.

For me? That was ball.

God, I loved sports. I was built for them. I was good at them, and I knew it, and I had a thirst for it—and I knew that too. It would be impossible not to. The feel of leather in my hands, my fingers between the laces. Barreling through a line, getting knocked on my ass until my teeth rattled in my head. Dribbling down a court and sinking a layup, hearing the swoosh of the net when the ball melted through the hoop like it was nothing. All of it was joy. It was life.

But none of that mattered.

Not next to the kingdom we were building for the Lord.

I begged my parents to let me play. All through middle school, that was all I wanted. Keep me inside for dances, make me go to church every damn day, but please, *please* let me play ball.

The answer was no.

We couldn't afford it, not really. And I knew that. I got it to some degree, as much as you can when you're a kid. That was one reason behind it, and it wasn't a bad one. But the real one, the one they harped on, the one they believed in down to their bone marrow was that they couldn't have their boy mingling with the world.

"Just because we live in this world, Don, doesn't mean we have to be *of* this world."

I didn't even know what that meant, and neither do half the folks who spit it out. I lived in the world! My friends lived in the world! My parents lived here, too, and there was nothing we could do to change that. (There was nothing I *wanted* to do to change it, but I wasn't about to say that out loud. Not yet, anyway.) But that was the refrain. It was everywhere in scripture, wasn't it?

> *If you belonged to the world, it would love you as its own.*
> *As it is, you do not belong to the world, but I have chosen*
> *you out of the world. That is why the world hates you.*[3]

> *Do not love the world or anything in the world. If anyone*
> *loves the world, love for the Father is not in them.*[4]

> *You adulterous people! Do you not know that friendship*
> *with the world is enmity with God? Therefore whoever*
> *wishes to be a friend of the world makes himself an enemy*
> *of God.*[5]

---

3   John 15:19—NIV
4   1 John 2:15—NIV
5   James 4:4—NIV

It was right there, in black and white. Red and white, depending on your translation. And that meant it was inarguable. I didn't want to be an enemy of God, did I? I didn't really want *friendship with the world.* And playing ball—not just messing around at the park, but really capital P *Playing Ball*? That guaranteed it—I was lost. I was going to be part of the world if I did that. Did I want that?

Of course I did!

Frankly, I hit a point where I didn't really care. It didn't matter to me if I was going to be an enemy of God. What I wanted was to play. What I wanted was to live. I would have been playing ball with the same kids I met at the park to hoop with every day, the same kids my little brother would spy on me when I was around. That was the world, right? Was *this* what was supposed to be so bad?

Fine.

Good.

I liked the world. I loved it.

If all this was right, if all this theology and scripture and mission we were on meant anything, then the world was what we were supposed to be saving anyway. Not that I cared much about that, when it came down to it. But it didn't make any sense, and *that* I cared about. How was I supposed to dedicate my whole life to saving the world but never fall in love with it?

All I wanted. Was to play. Ball.

The answer was no.

The answer was: you should want the kingdom of God to grow. You should want to be saved.

I thought about that long and hard. I had a whole lifetime to think about it. To resent it. To want to dive into life and experience it and be told that was wrong. That there was one person I was allowed to be, one thing I was allowed to want. And one day, I just…didn't anymore.

I'll never forget the day I hopped in the station wagon and looked my dad right in the eye; I was finally tall enough to do that at sixteen years old. I had things I wanted to do. Ball I wanted to play. But I had to miss it, like I always did. We weren't balling today. We were going to church.

I threw my hands up and snapped. This was it; this was *really* it. "Well," I said, "if I can't, I don't wanna be saved no more."

My dad glanced over and blinked. Then he chuckled. He wasn't a loud man; he was cool and collected, and that didn't change even in the face of something like this. It just didn't track, see? No one didn't want to be saved, not when they really had it in their fingers. Certainly not his son. He said, through half-laughter and a gospel quartet in the background, "Boy, something's wrong with you." Then he moved into church talk. "The devil is a lie. You *are* saved. Me and my household, we shall serve the Lord, and you are my son, and you are saved."

"If this is what it is, if this—if all this nothing is what it takes for me to saved, then I don't want it. I can't play ball. I can't go to dances. I can't play in the bands that aren't drums at church. And if this is what I've gotta do to be saved, I. Don't. Want it."

Talk about waves. My parents didn't know what to do with me after that; I wasn't just a kid who didn't understand. I did, and my answer was no.

I think it was that moment that prompted my father to start looking inside himself, start loosening the reins just a little. In the ninth grade, I was allowed to hang out at the football games. I never did get to play football, and that's something that cuts to this day when I think about it. But at least I could *go*. I was allowed to play basketball. And that was something.

It was all of this that cause my dad to one day finally look at me, lay down the belt for good, and say, "I'm not doing this anymore. I'm just—I'm gonna pray for you, Don."

Fine by me.

Fine. By. Me.

CHAPTER THREE

I GREW UP AROUND A WHOLE LOT OF FOLKS WITH NAMES THAT would go on to mean something. I played ball with a kid named Wayman Tisdale, the kind of kid who people were coming from all around the country to watch ball. Scouts would roll in and watch that boy shoot hoops right there in Cheyenne Park. But more important than that, to my family at least, was that his daddy was a preacher. Now, to my dad, everything was a "no" before it was a "yes." I was familiar with that (why do you think I became a promoter?), so when I watched Wayman, son of Pastor Tisdale, playing basketball at the park and on the team, I knew he was a potential way to "yes."

Now he was more than that to me; Wayman was an honest-to-god friend. He played bass, I played drums. He played ball, and so did I. We connected in the way that only two preacher's kids can. And he helped me out, whether he knew it or not. I'd tell my dad, "Look! How can playing ball be a sin? Wayman's playing!" If Wayman was playing, surely I could play. We got there eventually, and Wayman *really* got there. He played ball at OU, then went on to play pro ball for the Sacramento Kings and a few other teams. From there, he made a name for himself, finding stardom in the jazz scene. It was Wayman who produced one of the first ever records on my label—a jazz album for my brother, Eldredge Jackson.

And Cheyenne Park? They eventually renamed that for a boy we used to hang around and shoot hoops with every day—John Starks. He went on to play for the New York Knicks during the Michael Jordan era of sports.

But the name that meant more to me than anything was ID Wilson. Charlie Wilson, of the Gap Band, was ID's son, and that turned out to mean a whole lot in my life. ID, see, was a member of the Church of God in Christ, just like we were. And she was *bold*. That woman knew exactly what she wanted and how to get it, and for whatever reason, she decided to bring me along for the ride.

Now I couldn't play drums anywhere but church. I could sneak around to my friends' garages and play, but my drum set wasn't even really mine. My siblings had their instruments they could move around with them wherever they went, but mine? Those drums were the church's. So it wasn't like I was a performer; I didn't get the chance to be. But I practiced whenever I could in those little garage bands, and I played my heart out at church. And Irma Dean Wilson noticed me.

ID, whom everyone called Mother Wilson, was the state supervisor of the musical department in the Church of God in Christ. She'd done everything she could to get her son's career up and running, but Charlie had just gotten his first record deal. Charlie Wilson and the Gap Band was taking off. So Mother Wilson was looking for another project, and I was it.

She took me everywhere. She saw something in me and made me her drummer. I was playing all over the country, because I was Mother Wilson's drummer. That was what kept me going. I might not have been able to play on the drumline or in bands that weren't singing about Jesus, but I was *playing*. There's nothing stronger in the heart of an artist than the need to create, and because of Mother Wilson, I was allowed to create.

I had an outlet.

And then, a few years into my father's preaching career, right before I went off to college, my father veered off from the Church of God in Christ and went independent. This shouldn't have been a big ordeal, but I'll be the first to tell you: church people are a mess.

Mother Wilson ran an organization called the PSMA, which provided scholarships for kids in the denomination. I'd been playing for years, banking on that. But the second we left, the church let her know that she couldn't give it to me anymore. I wasn't part of the church, regardless of whether I had a say in it.

Now, that wasn't gonna fly with ID. She stood her ground, said, "Absolutely not. That's my son, and I'm giving him every cent I said I would."

By God, she did.

Mother Wilson was the one who took me to my first ever Charlie Wilson and the Gap Band concert. I went with the mama, so I got VIP status. Not only did she give me the gift of music, she taught me how to promote. I'd help her pass out flyers and bring in listeners for her musicals, and she told me I could do anything or be anything. She told me I'd play for her son when I got older, and I believed I would.

Now, I didn't play for the Charlie Wilson and the Gap Band. But I sure managed the career of Robert Wilson, one of their members, and I produced their 25th anniversary celebration.

God gave me the opportunity to see the behind-the-scenes bullshit that went on inside a church building.

Mother Wilson gave me freedom.

And I think it was that taste, that woman's influence and that years-long period of my life, that allowed me to really truly shake the chains of my upbringing when I pushed the gas pedal to the floor, left my little town behind, and went off to college.

CHAPTER FOUR

LEAVING HOME IS ALWAYS ABOUT MORE THAN MOVING HOUSE.

Some folks pack up, go off to school, get themselves a bunch of friends and a fancy degree, come back, and are content to stay just the same as they were before. But for a lot of us, we head out into the world, and we use that as a chance to come back different.

I didn't just pack up. I *left home*.

College was a time of immense growth for me—personally, academically, spiritually. All the major ways someone can change, I did. That's the way it happens for so many of us, right? I'll never forget how it felt to leave the dust of my hometown behind and pick up new dirt in my treads. But none of that happened overnight. Change almost never does.

I'd left my hometown knowing that, when it came to my church, there were things I connected with and things I didn't. Things I believed and things I never would. I knew things were about to change. And maybe that was *why* it took a little while to sink in: I was prepared for it. I wasn't in a rush; I'd always been Don the Prodigal, and I was happy to quietly stay that way for a while.

I couldn't even point you to one singular event. One lecture, one friend who really shifted everything for me.

I don't have a dramatic story from my time in school, a Pauline moment that I can pull out to display as the second the scales fell away from my eyes.

That's not my story. My story is one of slow realization. Of a freedom that came from moving out of my parents' town into my own.

Slowly, little by little, I started to see the world differently.

Now, I was still a Christian. At this point, we were no longer a part of the Churches of God in Christ, remember—my family had gone independent. But that faith was still a part of who I was, warts and all. It had given me hard things, but I can say now that it had also done right by me from time to time, and I didn't want to throw the baby out with the bath water the second I got out on my own. I might not have agreed with everything I'd been taught, but Jesus was still all I knew. So that's what I chose to believe.

The difference was, I was doing it on my own terms. And the longer I got outside, the longer I got to chew on that intellectual freedom, the more my beliefs began to shift. It became extremely clear to me that I wasn't in the minority for believing the way I did, for wanting to really *live* in the moment in my life, for not buying that God worked in the restrictive, exclusionary way I'd been raised to believe He did. In one move, my world exploded from a little church in a little town into a full globe. And once that can of worms is opened, no one's ever getting it put back in.

My behind-the-scenes experience in the church didn't exactly help bring me back into the fold. After school, I went back to my hometown, where my dad's church had become by sister's church. And family was real and permanent no matter what happened, no matter what crazy thing Don was believing that week, so of course, I attended. I didn't need to agree with everything they taught to go and enjoy my family and the friendship and community that come with a tightly knit church.

But I knew. I knew how things worked, both in front of and behind that pulpit. When I moved to L.A. and dove into my career—promotion, I never did find a church to be a part of. I didn't need to; that wasn't who I was anymore. My beliefs had already evolved to a different plane. And being real? I recognized too much church in the promoting game.

Maybe it was the other way around. I didn't use what I learned in promotion to back engineer it into a doctrine, into deciphering what I'd watched in the church. But I used what I learned in church to win at promotion.

And I did it well.

It's supposed to be about God and Jesus and loving each other, and I truly believe that for a lot of folks, it really is. Most people inside the church are good. They want to do what's right. They want to live just lives and help their fellow man. But you get into the nitty gritty of the way churches work, and things start to look a whole lot different.

It's all a money game! The congregants give to the pastor, and the pastor gives to the bishop, and the bishop gives, and eventually, you start to realize that when it comes right down to it, it's about the money. Love offerings for the music minister and the guest preacher and the youth minister, and so on and so forth. The money changes hands one way or another, but at the end of it all, it always winds up funneling up. No matter how much I believed that God ought to be taking care of us financially too, it never seemed to materialize. That cash in the offering plate went to fund something bigger, like it always does.

And that wasn't the congregation.

Like I said, it was the church that taught me the hustle. It taught me people. It taught me to promote. What it didn't teach me was how to live, and what it meant to *really* value both this life, and unity with people.

What finally pushed me into that was what happened to me six years ago: my heart attack.

PART TWO:

NOW

CHAPTER FIVE

THERE'S NOTHING LIKE SHAKING HANDS WITH DEATH TO WAKE you up to the reality of life. Before my heart stopped, I'd been pondering. I'd spent my whole life pondering what was real, what it all meant, where my parents had gone wrong and where they'd gone right. What made sense, what jived with the things I could taste and touch and see, and what didn't. I'd spent an existence building a foundation for this change. But then, it happened—I felt what it was to die. Or awfully close to it.

Talk about hurtling into clarity.

I was rushed to the hospital, into emergency surgery, and I saw it all. I saw the doctors working on me, heard them asking for a scalpel and playing music during the procedure. I watched myself on the operating table and then again when I slowly started to come out of it and back to the world. I didn't die. But I skirted close enough to the cliff's edge that I had no choice but to reevaluate.

And the conclusion I came to was this: we're wrong.

We're wrong; that's the long and short of it.

Somewhere along the line, the philosophy we've adopted as a species has gone off the rails, and you and I both know that whatever it is we're trying to do isn't working. When I saw my life flash before my eyes, when I watched my quiet body being cut open, what I wasn't thinking about was division. I wasn't a solitary being, just pure and simple "Don", like I'd always been. Like all of us have been taught to think we are.

I was part of everything. Science knows that that's a fact, but folks, I *felt* it.

And that's it: that's where we've veered off the track.

If we were right about these little squabbles, these ideas about who God is and what He wants, what He doesn't want, whether "He" is even the right word—if we were right that it was the most pure and righteous command to keep our sons out of basketball and our butts in pews on Sunday morning, we wouldn't turn on the news to smoking ruins every morning.

Look around. What do you see? Sickness. War. Fighting. Brother against brother. Racism. Bigotry. Betrayal. Death.

What we all want is peace. We want a world where love prevails and we all work toward a common purpose, where our children can ride their bikes down the street or head off to school and we don't have to worry that they won't be coming home that night.

What we are doing to get it?

It isn't working.

Now, take that picture you've got—the grainy one full of chaos and despair, and refocus it. Look a little closer, and what you'll see are people fighting for each other, between those moments of madness. You'll see folks cleaning up after acts of violence, holding each other's hands and taking care of their neighbors. Look close enough, and you'll see God peeking through the cracks. I'm not talking about an old man with a beard and a golden scepter on a throne in the clouds. I'm talking about the only God there is, about the energy holding the universe together, about the very basics we're about to get back to in this book, and, I hope, in this world: I'm talking about unity.

The moments in which we as a people can truly see the tiniest glimpses of the world we want to build are the moments when we remember, for an instant, who we are. When we remember that none of this is about you or me or your neighbor with the annoying dog—that it's not about you and me as individuals, and it never was. It's not you and me. It's *us*.

Let's go back to where it all started. Now I wasn't there when the cosmos came into being. I wasn't—and I was. Don wasn't there, with his love for the Saints and good bourbon. But I was, because *we* were.

If we understood that the whole meaning of this adventure on planet earth had nothing to do with ourselves, and everything to do with who we *all* are, if we could understand that birth isn't something new springing into existence and death isn't something slipping out of it, if we knew that we are just a piece of God and in the end, we'll go right back to being a part of that whole, maybe—just maybe—none of us would be so concerned with building our own little empires, whatever those look like. We wouldn't have to build our own networks and scheme and hurt others for the sake of getting ahead. We would understand that we are one and the same, and that in the end, in the beginning, in the middle where we are right now, that's the only thing that matters.

The largest living organism on planet earth is a grove of quaking aspen trees in the Utah mountains. It's called the Pando Aspen Clone—the trembling giant. A single organism that has spread over 106 acres of land. It looks like thousands and thousands of trees. But beneath the surface, all of those trees share a single root system. They're thousands of expressions of one living creature.

The trembling giant is dying.

That organism has stood for centuries, but a combination of human encroachment and animals grazing on individual pieces of the Pando—those trees that pop above ground and fool us into thinking they could exist on their own—is slowly killing it.

Humanity—you and I, if we worked together, if we understood that we are connected by a single root system, we could be a trembling giant. As it stands, we live on our own, humans and nature chipping away at our greatest strength: our unity. Our forgotten knowledge that at the root of it, God is all of us, and we are God.

And we are not alone.

If we can understand that, if we can remember it—we can change the world.

CHAPTER SIX

WHERE IT ALL BEGINS IS THIS: PRECONCEPTION.

There are two forces on this earth, and while we're all walking around taking for granted that they are one and the same, the fact is that they're not. They're fighting entities, and we are caught in the middle.

Those two entities are: perception and reality.

Now, what I'm saying isn't new. It's thousands of years old. It goes all the way back to the Greeks—to Plato himself. So let me just put on a toga and some of those olive branches behind my ears and philosophize at you. We're going to have a symposium.

Plato had a lot of big ideas—fitting, because he was a big guy. The man didn't philosophize under a noble name; he taught under his wrestling name. That's right; before Plato carved out his place as one of the greatest thinkers of our time, he was making a living doing pro-wrestling. And that name? Plato? It was Greek for "broad." This man who walked the streets of Greece under the name "BIG" wrote so much of what we now believe about human consciousness, and that might seem irrelevant, but it isn't. Nothing is. If we can believe that both philosophy and killer wrestling moves came from the body of the same man, then maybe we can start to believe that humanity and plants and animals and existence all come out of the same God.

More than that, Plato was a common man. He wasn't spitting out words from on high, feeding philosophy to academics from the peak of a mountain.

Plato was just an athlete, a guy who liked to wrestle and think—a human like you or me. And he *understood* this.

That counts for something in my book.

One of the most important things Plato came up was something called the cave allegory. Before we can even start to understand God, nature, the building blocks of existence, and finally, how we can use that to change ourselves and then the entire world, we've got to understand this. Because this, my friends, is the key.

Plato saw humanity as bound, to begin with. Trapped in a dark cave—one we were born in, and one most of us would die in. All we know is darkness and cold and the endless dripping of water from the stalactites—not that we'd have any occasion to know what they're called. In front of us is a fire, and behind us, we don't know. We're chained, dark and smoke in our eyes.

Because we've never had the reason or the opportunity to look behind us, "behind" doesn't exist. But it *does*, objectively. And if we could only break out of those chains, we could see that beyond the mouth of the cave behind us is reality. That there is real, vibrant life just beyond our reach. But we can't. So all we're left with is the shadows that those pieces of reality cast on the cave walls in front of us.

To us, this is real.

This is all life is.

The real world is nothing but a thin shadow of itself.

That is perception.

There's a psychological concept called "belief perseverance." This is the phenomenon in which someone has held onto a belief for so long that even when confronted with irrefutable evidence to the contrary, that person must reject it in order to hold onto what they know.

Plato—the original Notorious B.I.G.—got that too. He said people were so attached to their caves, to that shadow-dancing on the wall they called life, that even if someone showed up with a key and unlocked their chains and said, "Hey. None of this is what's real. I've got something so much better for you," it wouldn't work. People would get angry, they'd get violent.

Belief perseverance. That's the real enemy here.

We're so afraid of change, so afraid of the unknown, that we'd rather live thin lives of shadow than accept that maybe there's something better in store—because *better* means *different.*

I don't know that there's a scarier word in the English language than "change." We do everything we can to run from it. Sometimes it's small, it's a haircut we put off for three months because we're just not sure we're ready to move from a #3 razor to a #2. But sometimes it's big. Sometimes it's a move across the country or a change in vocation.

And sometimes, it's the biggest one of all. It's more than a change in geography. It's a change in belief. A change in *mind.* That's the *real* scary stuff. Because once you allow your mind to begin to change, the earth starts to move underneath you. The beliefs that held you steady in reality, the dirt beneath your feet, it all becomes shifting sand. You're forced to confront not only a future that's morphed from a perfectly ordered photograph into a hazy charcoal, but also a past that's colored in a whole lot differently than you remember.

You've got to rethink conversations you had, relationships that ended or began, you've got to rethink your present and your future and everything about yourself.

Most people don't make it this far.

Change is scary.

It's a fact: most people would rather be comfortable than happy—even if that comfort means being stuck in something unsatisfying. Or in our case, in a dangerous world, one full of sadness and chaos and billions of people who think they're doing it right while the world burns down around them.

But we are brave people.

And if someone shows up with a key, we are going to take it ourselves and look behind us to see what lies beyond the mouth of that cave.

And we are going to dive into a brand new world we don't understand, because it's real.

We are going to be brave enough to *redefine*, and we are going to start right now.

CHAPTER SEVEN

THE FIRST THING WE'VE GOT TO TALK IS SCIENCE.

Now, science and religion don't often mix. I was taught growing up, and I think a lot of us were, that science was in one corner and faith was in another. If we were really going to believe in God, then sure, science was valuable. Studying God's creations meant studying God. Looking at the trees and the wildlife and the way the world spun wasn't useless, but it was inferior.

It had to be!

Too much of what so many of us grew up believing ultimately puts concepts into a hierarchy, and it pits science and faith against one another. Eventually, it insinuates, you will run across a piece of knowledge about the universe that will force you to choose: science or faith? And faith had to win out. Faith, we believed, means seeing one thing with your eyes, but choosing to believe in something different.

I don't want to ask you to do that. Folks, *I* can't do that. I can't see the data on something and shut my eyes to it, no matter how much doing so might enrich my life. And this isn't a knock on people who can. Some of the best people I've ever known have been people of faith. But that isn't me, and it isn't something I'm going to ask you to do.

This is the first thing we've got to redefine—the relationship between faith and science. The fact is, faith was never about denial. It was never about a God who would show you one thing and require you to shut your eyes to it and believe another. Faith is just about belief; that's all it is. It's about making a leap, sometimes into the unknown, but never into the disproven. Faith is the firm belief in something or somebody, and I see no reason why that has to compete with science in any reality. If we are to have faith in something, science should support it, not do battle with it. Science should not act as a test to our faith, but as something that strengthens it, that proves it.

To that end, let's talk about the first idea I want to present here. The first claim that's going to sound a little nuts, a little far out, that's going to require us to bring in all the stuff we just talked about with our guy Plato. A willingness to throw out the old and bring in the new. But that's the only way we change. And changing ourselves is the only way we change the world. So we're going to take this idea, look at the science behind it, and run with it.

Principle I: Matter Doesn't Create Consciousness. Consciousness Creates Matter.

It sounds wild and impossible. Matter is everything you can touch, that you can see and experience with your own eyes. Matter is what makes up everything, right? So how on earth can it be that consciousness creates the living world and not the other way around? This is where you think, "Don's lying to me. He's telling me he's not going to make me choose between science and belief, and right off the bat, he says something crazy."

Stay with me.

I said I wasn't going to ask you to choose, and I'm a man of my word.

The fact of the matter (I'll let you decide whether that pun was intended) is that science actually *supports* this idea.

What is matter? For those of us who haven't graced a science classroom in a number of years, matter is the material substance that makes up the observable universe. Your house, your dog, the couch you're sitting on, the salt in the ocean, and the gas that powers your car—those are all made up of matter.

It's what you can touch—or is it?

Let's delve a little deeper. One of the more shocking revelations that science has given us in the past few decades is that you never *truly* touch anything. You don't. Some of us may have heard this and some of us haven't, but it's an unmitigable truth backed up by physicists' intimate understanding of the universe: we can never touch anything.

How is that?

Well, I'm sure you remember this from science class: we're all made up of molecules. And molecules are made up of atoms. Taking off another layer of this Russian nesting doll of scientific theory, atoms are made up of protons, neutrons, and electrons. In the nucleus, we've got protons and neutrons, but, and this is a critical *but*, outside the nucleus is where the important stuff happens—at least the important stuff to proving this idea. It's the electrons outside that nucleus that make it so that you can't really truly ever touch your couch or your dog or your Great Aunt Sally. Those electrons, see, are negatively charged. And anything that's charged negatively repels other negatively charged things. Like a magnet. You ever try to push two magnets together from the wrong side? They fight against it. That's electrons. Two things that just can't make it work together. That means that no two atoms can ever truly touch, because no electrons ever will.

If that's all that you and I and the universe are made of, then that's it, that's settles it. We'll never touch.

So why can I feel the chair I'm sitting on right now? Why does it hurt when I touch a stove or feel the softness on my hands when I run my fingers through my purring cat's fur?

Well that's it. That's the center of all of it—why do you *feel* when you can't *touch*? Perception.

And what is it that allows perception in the first place?

Consciousness.

This is where things start to get a little strange and where folks start to check out. Where they start to feel the pull toward the shadows on the wall and toward clinging to those as true reality, because anything else seems impossible. Like too big of a leap. But stay with me, and let's talk about it.

If what I feel—if what I taste and touch and see and smell and hear, what I *experience*, is reality, and if the thing that allows me to understand that at all is consciousness, then is it so wild to ask if perhaps it's consciousness that creates reality? That creates matter? Rather than the other way around?

Folks, the idea that the material world is all there is didn't even spring into common acceptance until the 1700s. Before that, the spiritual and the mental were interlaced in everything. It wasn't always decided. And importantly, it hasn't been updated since! We got this idea in our heads that the universe is built of matter, and that if somehow, somewhere, consciousness ceased to exist, what we'd be left with is lifeless bits of nothing floating around.

I don't even have to say this for you to know it's true: that's depressing. It sucks the meaning out of everything. And this sounds subjective—because it is—but it doesn't *feel* right. It doesn't feel right with what I know about the profoundness of experience. About the depths of passion and the heights of feeling. The idea that matter is there, floating around doing nothing, and my consciousness and yours just jumped into action one day for no reason, and when it's gone, things will keep floating by like nothing happened, well it doesn't sit right.

It especially doesn't sit right knowing that for years, we haven't been allowed to consider an alternative.

That's what I want to do here: I want to consider an alternative.

When we dive into the realm of quantum physics, suddenly, a host of possibilities we never imagined opens up.

I'm not a scientist, so I'm not about to write you an intricate science textbook here (those of us without doctorate degrees are breathing a sigh of relief…and those of you *with* them are doing the same thing. You don't want me teaching your twelve years of study and mucking it up, and I know it), but I want to talk about the biggest thing quantum physics has taught us, in normal human terms. And that is: there are tiny particles, particles that make up the particles that make up the particles that make up you and me. I'm talking about the building blocks *of* the building blocks of the universe. And those particles behave *differently* depending on how they're studied. We've proven it over and over, in the most impossible ways—in light behaving as a particle or a wave depending *solely* upon whether it is being observed by a conscious party. On two otherwise identical jars of rice being spoke to positively or negatively, and going down two completely different paths of existence and decay depending on that energy that was given to them. We can watch consciousness create reality right in front of us, and we *have*.

That's right; you can look it up. Ask your physics professor or hop onto Google right now and you'll find this. Pieces of the very nature of reality change how they behave depending on how they're being measured. We have real, concrete evidence that *our choices* affect the very nature of reality, the things that create matter itself.

That alone ought to set us to wondering, shouldn't it?

Shouldn't that discovery rock us back on our heels?

Shouldn't it make us begin to question whether the theory we have based our entire mainstream understanding of science on ought to have been updated some time in the last three hundred years?

The fact is that humans exerting their will on this object causes it to change course, and I, along with a number of scientists and engineers and the world's great thinkers, posit that that should tell us something about the nature of reality.

What is experience?

This one's not too bad. It's something you and I can understand. We know what it is to feel, to touch, to love, to hate, to be present. We know what experience looks like. But the biggest discovery here is that so many of us believe that experience only comes from brain waves. That it is all physical. Folks, I'm here to tell you that that is not true.

For the longest time, science has asserted that brain waves produce experience. But studies involving dream states, the experience of a heart attack or similar medical emergency, dissociative states, the specific kind of trip that comes from LSD or psilocybin—they all contradict this idea.

In fact, they show an increased dynamic and vivid experience with a *decrease* in brain activity.[6][7] Opposite of what we've all heard, right? The brain should light up when we are feeling things, experiencing mental stimulation. But in a number of cases, it *doesn't*.

So that means that experience cannot come exclusively from the brain. From physical stimuli. No, it's more than that. It is so, *so* much more, my friend.

What is consciousness?

We've got to do business with this concept now, before we tackle anything else. I've shown you the end of this leg of the race, so now that you've got an idea of where we're headed, let's jump back to the starting line for a second.

What is consciousness, anyway?

Consciousness is universal.

Consciousness is God.

---

6   https://vimeo.com/492514077 Essentia Foundation
7   https://www.youtube.com/watch?v=RtOXx84aT-c Dr. Bernardo Kastrup, Essentia Foundation

Consciousness is the most formative building block of the universe—a fundamental force that exists. From consciousness comes life and energy and real experience—life. To live is more than just to vaguely experience. A house experiences. A house experiences being built from cement and wood, being constructed into a skeleton and getting its skin—its insulation, its drywall, its fancy sheen of paint. A house experiences nails being driven into its roof and doors being installed, and, the contractor hopes, a house experiences being lived in. Scuffs on the walls, the dog knocking into the door every time the postman rings, the wine being spilled on the carpet.

If *walls could talk*, they say.

But they can't.

The walls experience, but they don't know they do.

That's the next step.

It was Descartes who gave us the famous phrase, "I think, therefore I am."

We hear it all over the place, but we don't know exactly what it means, most of us. We don't stop to think about that, because we, like the walls, are too busy experiencing a thousand other things (things like the wine on the carpet and the scuffs on the walls, am I right?). But what *does* it mean? It means that existence, that consciousness, comes from thought. Not from the simple fact of experiencing without knowledge or analysis.

To *be* means to *know*.

The second stage of existence comes not just from experiencing being hit with a basketball upside your head, but knowing that it hurts. Knowing that you're pissed about it. And knowing that you *know*.

I do not just feel. I know I feel.

And that is allowed for by consciousness.

So, then what?

If consciousness births the crossroads between knowledge and experience, and we agree that reality is more than dead matter, then we can build from that framework to the doozy we opened with: consciousness creates matter.

You know when you, for instance, take a sip of bourbon, that bourbon burns going down. You know that it's going to give you a funny feeling in your limbs if you haven't eaten enough all day. You know that you like it, or that you don't. It is not the bourbon sitting there in the bottle that creates experience; it is your perception.

It is your acting upon that bourbon that shifts it into a different state, that *creates reality*.

It is your consciousness that gives you a full and varied experience, pervading your senses, when you take a sip of that bourbon, even though bourbon is nothing more than little molecules, and the energy binding it together with everything else.

So let's take that thought and use it as a foundation to build something irrefutable. That's a strong word, and as soon as I use it, I know I'm boxing myself in. But I don't mind that so much, not when this is so rock solid, so impossible to scientifically disprove. It is not a theory as much as it is a set of observations about the rules of the universe: consciousness creates matter.

How?

Because matter *itself* is an idea.

That feels wrong; it makes the universe suddenly feel unstable. Unreal. But think about this. Everything is just…what it is. Matter is a collection of molecules (a concept we came up with), and molecules are a collection of atoms (another concept we came up with), and atoms are a collection of protons and neutrons and electrons (another of ours), and protons are—

Are you starting to get it?

We, as conscious beings, saw the meaningless pieces around us and grouped them into meaningful things. A banana is not intrinsically a banana. That collection of molecules is a banana because we derive meaning and value out of calling it a banana.

The banana exists *as a banana* because we have chosen to make it so.

The water of the ocean and the clouds in the sky exist as separate things, as pieces of matter, because we decided that they did.

The answer to that age-old question: if a tree falls in the woods and there's no one there to hear it, does it make a sound? Is *NO!* No it does not. A tree can't create sound on its own; that happens in the eardrum. Sound exists because of perception.

And so it goes with matter.

We have thought matter into existence.

Matter is an idea, and so is the larger universe itself.

Further, I, and many other scientists contend, that it is that energy, that life force that runs through everything, that allow matter to function as it does.

The table and the floor and your television and your hair and the sky and the rocks—all those things may not be conscious, but they are held together by more than simple matter. They are molecules and subatomic particles held together by *energy.* It is in that energy, in that nearly infinite space between particles, that we can find meaning.

It is in human consciousness, then, that nature itself finds meaning. Before human consciousness, nature, the cosmos, all of that consciousness existed in a delirium of violence—cycling and going through periods of chaos and doing and undoing without knowing why. But in humanity, nature has freed itself from that delirium. In our consciousness, it finds its way into purpose and order and meaning.

Principle 2: The Universe Is God Experiencing Himself Through Us

Don, you're thinking. *That's bananas. You've moved from science and logic to something metaphysical and hippie-dippie and wild.*

Being real with you? I thought so too. Honestly, I don't know how I'd feel about a mind that accepted this right away with no further explanation. But there are holes in the plot of the universe as it sits, and this is the only theory I've found to truly stitch them back up.

Let's dive back into energy. It is invisible forces that hold every piece of matter in the universe together. It is energy. When you get right down to it, everything is made of energy; all of it. What makes up *most* of an atom, a molecule—what keeps it moving? What keeps it so that it doesn't go into immediate dead decay? Energy.

It is *all* energy, and energy is something we can't see. Can't touch, not really.

But it's working at all times to hold the universe together.

Like our friend matter, we can go two routes with that knowledge: energy is dead—it is nothing. An automaton that sprung forth from nothing and just happened to know what it needed to do. Dead energy holds together dead matter and you and I are made of death.

We, the universe, everything in it are dead things.

Or—*or*—we are made up of life.

We are vibrant and whole and moving, and so is the universe itself.

What it all comes down to is what we believe about the space between what we can touch (what we think we can touch). And let's be clear about that too: all religion, all faith, all systems of belief come down to this: puzzling out the spaces between the things we can touch. Right?

Faiths are there to explain the things we cannot see, and that is near verbatim scripture.

I may have been out of the church for a long time, but I still remember my Bible.

Hebrews 11:1 Now faith is being sure of what we hope for and certain of what we do not see.

It's right there. Right there in the force that holds everything together. That permeates *everything*—living and non-living.

Ask any person of faith what it is that holds the universe together? The answer is going to be God. No one believes in God without believing that He (or whatever pronouns make sense; binding God in the limits of language is a fool's errand) isn't the force that keeps it all running.

So what does that mean?

It means that God is energy.

God is the space between those tiny pieces, the living energy that makes the world run. God is more than just the fuel; God is the substance. God is in the *energy.*

And where is energy?

Everywhere.

We can prove that right there under the microscope; we have.

It's not even a leap of faith to connect these dots; it's a shuffle step. If God is that force, that God is energy, and if God is energy, then God lives everywhere.

God is in the dirt and the rocks and the sun and the coyote and the clouds—and God is in us.

Where this gets real, then, where this starts to *change* things, is that—going back to point 1—you and I are conscious. That means that God might live in a billion places, but that is meaningless if it cannot be experienced. We talked earlier about how consciousness is what enables experience, how it changes matter, how it ultimately creates it—and that is the crux of it right there: that we *experience* through consciousness.

God is energy, and God is in you and I.

And it is you and I who can touch and taste and breathe and hurt and hate and love.

You and I have God running through us. And it is you and I who allow *God* to experience everything He is holding together.

What is bigger, what is more revolutionary than that?

We are not dead space and dead energy and dead matter.

We are part of God.

I may not be a man of religion, but I am a man of faith. I am a man of *belief.* And that's why I wanted to write this in the first place—because real belief, real faith, changes lives. It changes the world. And if we only knew what we were made of, we could change everything.

CHAPTER EIGHT

THE QUESTION BECOMES: NOW WHAT?

For some of us, this means complacency. The idea that it doesn't really matter, right? It's not some currency-in/currency-out exchange. You put in enough good deeds, and you get a proportionate number of jewels on your crown at the end of it all.

So many of us were raised in really traditional Christian or Christian-derived religious structure, and we are still clinging to that idea in some way or another. The idea that what justice looks like is putting a certain amount of good in, and God making good on that investment when you get put in the ground. The great stock exchange in the sky.

And if that's not what's going to happen, then what's the point?

I get it. It's a fair question. It's a question that's *going* to come up when you live in the individualist capitalist society we work within. A society that motivates based on material benefit and entitlement—and I don't even use that word in a necessarily negative way. I'm talking about its root definition: the idea that if I do a certain thing, I am entitled to something in return.

I am.

Not *we* are.

I do this, and I ought to receive that.

This throws all of that out on its head, doesn't it? We've got a whole society functioning off this concept, and now something is coming along calling fully all of it into question.

But let me ask you this: *is* it functioning?

Is it?

In some ways, sure. We've got economies and social relationships and entertainment and places where we feel community and attachment. We've got a society that functions, in the barest of ways.

Now let's look a little deeper.

We've got economies—economies that war with one another for control. Even the most community-focused ones out there leave folks homeless, shivering and dying in the streets. Our social relationships are defined by arbitrary hierarchy. We've got shootings and racism and religious bigotry and a thousand things that have to make us wonder: is this working?

I contend that it's not.

I contend that the farther we get from the idea that we are all one, that the goodness and badness IRAs we're trying to set up for that final withdrawal are meaningless, those closer we come to delirium.

Delirium is how nature existed before meta-consciousness came into the world.

Take a look at your backyard. Deep within those blades of grass, that little ecosystem functions on a hundred acts of violence in an hour. The aphid eats sprouting, green life, and the ladybug eats the aphid, and the bird eats the ladybug. And on and on it goes. Nature is a struggle for resources, and without consciousness, that struggle always ends in violence. Natural life does not end in peace; it ends in pieces.

It has been this way since the beginning. The dinosaurs tore each other up, and life tears itself apart even now.

Nature functions off an instinctive program. And that program is *delirium*.

The persistence of nature is pushed forward by an impetus toward *life* and continued existence even in the face of enormous suffering. And without something to change that, to introduce an impetus toward something better, all of existence would simply go on like this forever.

But then humans showed up, and meta-consciousness entered the world. That evolved consciousness is what frees us from the natural delirium of unfettered nature. It gives nature the opportunity to form a new impetus, one that does not simply aim to persist in the face of suffering, but to persist and *avoid* suffering. What impetus can be greater than that?

Meta-consciousness, human consciousness, allows us the incredible gift of processing. We can not only think, but process our own thoughts. We can organize those thoughts into experience, into metacognition, into meaning.

Thought is comprised of images, little snapshots of memory and idea, and without consciousness, those snapshots are fragments—senseless, like a kaleidoscope. But we come along, and we get to put those together in a way that means something.

That is something to be handled not with callous thoughtlessness. It is not something to be taken for granted. That idea should be approached with reverence.

We have the ability to form a senseless machine into something with profound meaning, and in that ability—what a responsibility.

We just have to redefine what meaning looks like.

Goals Versus Meaning

One of humanity's biggest issues is conflating goals with meaning. We believe that it is our aims that give ourselves, give any actions we take, meaning. But friends, I think that's a mistake. A goal is something tangible. It is something to achieve.

I'd like to buy a house.

I'm going to marry the beautiful love of my life and have some kids.

I want to be the top achiever in my business.

Goals are good! Goals are healthy. They might help us in the pursuit of meaning, but they are *not* meaning in and of itself, and they are not what gives it to us.

Meaning does not come from something external, something we can control.

No, meaning is fundamental.

It is intrinsic.

Meaning is intimately and inextricably stitched into the fabric of existence, into conscious life, and it has nothing to do with what we are pushing to achieve individually. It just is.

We simply have to allow ourselves to approach that topic with new eyes.

Something with meaning, see, has worth. And do you not believe that God has worth? Do you not believe that *you* have worth? If you accept that God is in all of us, that we are in God, that we *are* the pieces of God that allow him to experience the world, then you have to allow it: you have meaning all on your own. With or without that house and car and perfect spouse. Without the job.

Meaning.

Is.

Inevitable.

And our lives, then, have meaning simply because they are.

Our lives have meaning because they are *gifts* to God, every one of them. Once we understand that the billions of us who exist now and existed then and will exist in the future allow God to experience creation, suddenly, a world and a life that can sometimes feel bereft is flooded with meaning.

Every insight we gain, every sensation we experience, every tiny drop of pain or gaping wound, every chuckle to the most all-consuming joy, gain and loss and feeling and tactile exploration—every bit of it is a contribution to all of us. To God. To a universal understanding and experience that leads to a fuller, more beautiful and whole God.

If your life is endless joy, that will contribute to consciousness.

If it is seemingly endless suffering, then that state of painful delirium helps evolve consciousness too, in the end.

Life, no matter what it looks like, serves a greater purpose than the small ones we have let ourselves be tricked into believing it serves.

And when we return to what we were before God dissociated, we are released into all of nature. We, and everything we gained and learned, and everyone gets *better*. We are together as one, in a beautiful collection of human experience across a vast landscape of time and space and feeling. Death is not a tragedy; it is a return.

Now, what I don't want to communicate is that in order to have value, we need to die. I don't want someone flashing this book around saying, "Well, I guess that settles it. To give to God, I'm gonna get into the business of serial killing."

I say this like it's ridiculous, like it's unthinkable. But for millennia, humanity has thought this way in one context or another. In ancient religions on every corner of the earth, and in cult gatherings, and in the minds of individuals, pleasing God had often equated to sacrifice. In order to make God happy, we must snuff out life—be those animal or human.

Conversely, religion can render life here useless. Because it is all about what comes next and what reward is garnered there, experiences here are dulled and rendered worthless. This is a piece of nothing, and taking joy in it is antithetical to hope and true enlightened spirituality. Experience on earth is rendered base and vulgar.

No. Neither of these can be true. Life is *precious*, every second of it we can experience.

The more we experience during our time on earth, the more insight we gain, and the more we can give back when our time here has ended.

If death is a harvest, then the fullest crops are the ones grown to their greatest potential, to the longest and richest points of their existence.

We owe it to ourselves and to God and to nature and to consciousness as a whole to live as long and vibrantly and intentionally as we can, so that at the end, we can build consciousness into something even more meaningful and knowledgeable and whole than it was before we were sent out on this journey into the ether.

Humanity, a while back, decided that death was the way to honor God. But the real gift to God is life, and everything in it. And death is the culmination of that.

It is this misunderstanding, and the delirium still present in the world, that makes it clear that we are not through evolving.

We have given nature the potential to push past suffering, but we have only been meta-conscious for a short time, and that means that we've got a lot of growing left to do.

So, What?

If this is all true—if meaning exists no matter the circumstances, no matter who you are. If your live and love and pain and heartbreak and joy are intrinsically meaningful. If it doesn't come down to a question of what God allows or of a reward-or pain-filled afterlife, if it doesn't all circle back to a benevolent creature in the sky or a set of rules we've got to live by—then *what*? What *does* it come down to?

It's up to us, isn't it?

It's up to us to live, in the most vibrant and beautiful ways possible.

To lap up experiences and passion like we are dying of thirst.

To link arms with every other piece of God on the planet and march together toward an existence that is closer to God and further from chaos and delirium.

To truly care about each other and the planet we inhabit and the God we come from, the pieces that we are.

If this is the way that existence and consciousness have manifested themselves, then we owe it to the universe, to each other, to ourselves—to live life with intention.

DON'S LETTERS TO
THE CHURCH(ES)

TO THE WHITE CHURCH:

[1] Don, a servant of the planet and the universe and everything and everyone in it

To all God's people in the white parts of the church

[2] Grace and peace to you from God our universal consciousness and all its segmented spirits:

The Claim

[3] The claim, the big lie that you've all been asked to believe by your preachers and your teachers and your televangelists waving their hands in the air on national television and asking you for money, is this, isn't it? [4] That the only reason that America is in the mess that it's in (and it is in a mess; on that we can all agree) is because we have *kicked God out of America*. It is because we as a collective have metaphorically burned the Bible on the altar of sin. [5] And if we would only go back to building a nation and a people off of the Bible as a foundation, everything would exist in peace.

[6] That claim, my friends. My dear brothers and sisters—and I *mean* that— is bullshit.

The Facts

[7] Let me remind you that it was the Bible-thumping Europeans who came across the ocean and desecrated 90% of the Indigenous population. It was in the pages of the Bible, in their white, European idea of God, that they got the justification for spreading horrific disease and raping and pillaging the people who were already here. [8] It was "Manifest Destiny" (an idea founded on God, on so-called *Biblical values*) that gave them license to barge into someone's home, massacre everyone there, and call it morality.

[9] *God was moving us to do this.*

[10] These are the people of your *Bible*, friends.

[11] It was the Bible that allowed your ancestors to travel to the shores of Africa and see Black folks not as human, but as a resource. To kidnap them from their homes and enslave them for their lives and the lives of their children and those children.

[12] See, the Bible dictates that if you are to enslave people from your own tribe, that can only last up to seven years. Why do you think that Europeans who came over under the control of another human only did so as indentured servants? [13] It is because the Bible allows for chattel slavery, as long as those slaves come from another nation. [14] It is your Bible that gave them more than one leg to stand on when they claimed leave to wrap a woman in chains, shove her in the belly of a slave ship, and lay claim to her and to the generations that came after.

[15] It is your Bible, in a sidebar about fabric blends and prohibitions on it, that let people determine that if a Black man married a white woman, or a white woman married a Black man, that ought to be illegal.

[16] It is your Bible that says that gay people ought to be stoned. That women ought to be silent, subservient to their husbands.

[17] That an adulterer should be stoned. That slaves should be obedient to their masters, for the sake of Jesus.

[18] That if a child is found to be disobedient, he ought to be killed.

[19] It is your Bible that says these things.

[20] It is not *taking the Bible out of America* that has gotten us into this brutal web of chaos in which this country exists. What made the mess of America is the supremacy that people have. [21] The audacity to think (and put into written, legal word) *I am better than you*. Because of technology or the color of my skin.

[22] At the time, that audacious supremacy was allowed. Because there was a vocal, powerful majority, and a minority that was not able to truly stand up for their damn rights.

[23] To say, *Hell no. We aren't going to allow this anymore!* Black people, other racial or cultural minorities, women, all of whom the Bible allowed the subjugation of, did not have the opportunity and environment to be able to stand up and truly *fight* for what they were owed—for the rights as humans.

[24] What you are seeing now in this country, the unrest you are so afraid of, the conflict, is not about the Bible. It's not about kicking God out of America— how can it be? You and I are God's eyes and ears and fingertips. [25] It is the pain that comes from change. It is people finally having the tools and ability to stand up and say, *We are not going to suffer under supremacy.* [26] It's not about God. It's not about the Bible. It is about making moves, critical moves, to a society that functions equally.

[27] But don't say this is about going back to the Bible. Making the Bible great again or what have you. Don't say it's about God.

[28] That is, and you can quote me on this, white people shit.

TO THE BLACK CHURCH:

[1] Don, a servant of the planet and the universe and everything and everyone in it

To all God's people in the white parts of the church

[2] Grace and peace to you from God our universal consciousness and all its segmented spirits:

You, And All That Comes With It

[3] You, who have gotten this far, you, who are a member of the Black church in America, and especially of the Church of God in Christ—the church I grew up in, the one I grapple with the most and love the hardest—you are a brave, *brave* soldier. And I am sure that by now, you're feeling some kind of way. [4] That which I say moving forward I say only with love. And you know the kind of love I'm talking about. I'm talking about the kind that comes from *kin.* That comes from the folks who know your laugh and what makes you angry, who know your favorite foods and that embarrassing thing you did when you were ten years old. [5] For you, I speak from the kind of love that comes from sharing in a thousand potlucks and looking down the pew to see who else was joining me in doodling on a visitor's card and whose mom was going to secretly pass a stick of gum down the aisle. [6] That kind of love is that kind that can speak to you. The kind that can pull you aside and ask you to consider a life shift, because you know that that person? The one who *knows* you, comes to you with nothing but a desire for you to live in the fullest happiness and purpose you possibly can. [7] That, my friends, is how I want you to see me coming.

The Pulling Aside

[8] If you're still reading, something is pulling at you. Maybe your upbringing is telling you it's nothing but the pull of the void. It's something to rear back

from, to decry as false, toss in the trash, and move on. [9] But even if that's what your spirit is telling you, friend, I don't think that can be it. Something is moving you forward and asking you to keep reading, to keep thinking, to keep asking while everything you've everything believed is being challenged. [10] That's hard. But it's real. Because the fact is that by now, you know that everything you've ever been taught is in direct contradiction to the arguments I've laid out. [11] So what's left?

[12] I'll tell you. It's not *Believe in Don*. Not only will I not ask you to take me at my word, I'll ask you not to. Don't believe me! All that mindset can lead to is more suffering, more rejection of critical thought and stepping further and further from who we are meant to be. [13] Take Jesus first. Yeah, I said it. Take Jesus by the hand—he's your best friend, you can do this together. [14] You take him by the hand and you choose to take a new path, a scary one. And on that path, you're going to ask yourself to do nothing but consider. I am asking you not to be afraid of questions. And more than that, not to be afraid of answers. [15] Whether they are mine or yours or something altogether different, something that none of us expected—to ask a question is bravery. And a question, an answer, can only ever strengthen something that is real and right.

[17] I am not trying to save you. That's not my job, and if it were, it would be an impossible one. Why? [18] Because you're fine. I don't need to save you; you're already saved, my friend. You're alright. You are meaningful. Whether you know it or not. [19] I'm not trying to save you; I'm trying to share information with you. Because in this life? For the purposes of this small, beautiful existence? [20] Only you can save yourself. And saving yourself looks like this: [21] *Now there is no condemnation for anyone. You are peace and happiness. Therefore, judge no man. Do not even judge yourself. Moderate yourself—there is a difference. Be and do what makes you happy. Mind your own business.* [22] Wait a second; I think my mic was turned low, so let me repeat that for the people in the back? *Mind. Your own. Business.*

[23] Before, there was division. There was meaning ascribed to the concept of us and them. Of you and me. But within the context of this new paradigm shift, those divisions and that concepts that make up their foundations melt away. [24] All dogmas become meaningless. They will disappear, and you, my friend, will see that there is only one being. There is only one God, and that God is consciousness, and everything. It is us; we are all part of *one* course and one purpose that matters.

[25] There are two factors at play, not a thousand like we have all believed. The truth? There is witness. And there is everything else. And all that is is the play of consciousness—that narrative that we perceive is real. [26] It is an illusion, just like a play on the stage. A story and an illusion being played out in God's mind. But even then, that is too limiting. [27] The last thing I want to do is to limit God, and I think that's the last thing you want, too. You and I both know that God is big. [28] And in God's mind, there is no division even for matter and concept. He simply *is*. He simply *experiences*. [29] His mind is peace and completeness and silence. Because God is not defined by what humans give meaning. He is so much more than that. [30] To describe God is to say too much. [31] God is ultimately a movement, and a rest. [32] God is love on the outside, and beauty on the inside.

[33] And, my dearest friend, so are you.

A NEW SET
OF COMMANDMENTS

YOU AND I ARE LIVING IN THE FUTURE. IN THE WORLD OF QUICK time and heaven in the metaverse, right? We function as avatars in the same playground of energy, and there's a lot of it to steal our attention. So I'm going to be brief here. In this economy, I' not going to throw out the full ten. I'm gonna hit you with seven commandments.

See? Efficiency.

Pin them on your bathroom mirror or set them as your desktop wallpaper, but take these things to heart, and watch your heart *change.*

The Seven Slightly Updated Commandments

1. Love everyone as yourself.

2. Judge no one.

3. Mind yo own damn business.

4. Do what makes you happy—because happiness is you.

5. You are not a separate self. Act like it.

6. God doesn't need your money and never did. Take that 10% and invest it, and you'll get a better return.

7. When in doubt, remember commandment number five.

FINAL REVELATIONS

MY FRIENDS, WE LIVE IN A FRIGHTENING WORLD. I CAN'T TELL YOU if it's always been this way, but I can tell you (and you already know) that it's overwhelming. We as people are desperately trying to find peace and belonging in a life constantly barraged with conflict and suffering. And with the rise of technology and instant communication, we have access to information about it at all times.

We see police violence. Shootings in schools. Trumpism and waves of intolerance and violence sweeping over folks like a wildfire. The rising tide of fascism that never *did* go away no matter how badly we wanted it to. Autocracy and wickedness across the board, resulting in some of the most devastating wars and bloodshed in history.

The fact is that consciousness is still young. We have not achieved peace yet, but consciousness is still in the process of correcting itself, and we are a part of it.

But there is one witness: that witness is God.

This is nothing but a story being played out for the mind of God. It is an illusion. Death and suffering and division are illusions, because at the end of it all? It's all God.

God is the player and the scene and witness.

We are the playing pieces that make up *God* experiencing himself, and isn't that overwhelmingly beautiful?

If we can remember that, then little by little, we can help build our existence, build *God's* experience, into something vibrant and dynamic and stunning.

You and I can remember to live for each other, and in doing so, live for God.

And that? Friends?

That is how we change the world.